homie

Also by Danez Smith

[insert] boy

Don't Call Us Dead

homie

/ poems /

DANEZ SMITH

GRAYWOLF PRESS

This publication is made possible, in part, by the voters of Minnesota through a Minnesota State Arts Board Operating Support grant, thanks to a legislative appropriation from the arts and cultural heritage fund. Significant support has also been provided by Target, the McKnight Foundation, the Lannan Foundation, the Amazon Literary Partnership, and other generous contributions from foundations, corporations, and individuals. To these organizations and individuals we offer our heartfelt thanks.

Published by Graywolf Press
250 Third Avenue North, Suite 600
Minneapolis, Minnesota 55401

www.graywolfpress.org

Published in the United States of America

ISBN 978-1-64445-010-9

2 4 6 8 9 7 5 3 1
First Graywolf Printing, 2020

Library of Congress Control Number: 2019933271

Cover design: Carlos Esparza

note on the title

this book was titled *homie* because i don't want non-black people to say *my nig* out loud.

this book is really titled *my nig*.

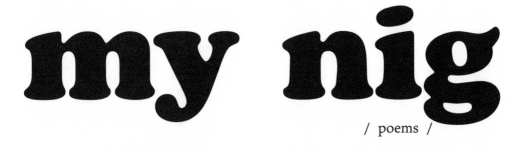

/ poems /

DANEZ SMITH

GRAYWOLF PRESS

Contents

for the homies
who keep me

for the realest one
Phonetic One
Andrew Thomas

for you & your friends

Yes, each man is a tower of birds, I write my friends
into earth, into earth, into earth.

ILYA KAMINSKY

Lost some real niggas I knew from a long time ago
But heaven or hell I hopin' that they be where I'mma go

LIL WAYNE

my president

today, i elect jonathan, eleven & already making roads out of water
young genius, blog writer, lil community activist, curls tight
as pinky swears, black as my nation   i trust the world in his tender
blooming hands, i trust him to tell us which rivers are safe to drink
& which hold fish like a promise

    & i elect eve ewing, who i know would ms. frizzle the country
    into one big classroom where grandmas finger paint
    the national budget & uncles stand around smoking blacks
    plotting on stars for our escape   she could walk to the podium
    at her inauguration & say, *the future is now,* & we'd all marvel
    at the sun & moon looping the sky like a gif as the cars learned
    to fly & our skin grew bulletproof

& colin kaepernick is my president, who kneels on the air
bent toward a branch, throwing apples down to the children & vets

        & rihanna is my president, walking out of global summits
        with wineglass in hand, our taxes returned in gold
        to dust our faces into coins

    & my mama is my president, her grace stunts
    on amazing, brown hands breaking brown bread over
    mouths of the hungry until there are none unfed

      & my grandma is my president & her cabinet is her cabinet
      cause she knows to trust what the pan knows
      how the skillet wins the war

        & the man i saw high kicking his way down the river?
        he is my president

& the trans girl making songs in her closet, spinning the dark
into a booming dress? she too is my president

& shonda rhimes is my president

& nate marshall is my president

& trina is my president

& the boys outside walgreens selling candy
for a possibly fictional basketball team are my presidents

& the bus driver who stops after you yell *wait!* only twice
is my pres

& the dude at the pizza spot who will give you a free slice
if you are down to wait for him to finish the day's fourth prayer
is my president

& my auntie, only a few months clean, but clean
she is my president

& my neighbor who holds the door open when my arms
are full of laundry is my president

& every head nod is my president

& every child singing summer with a red sweet tongue is my president

& the birds

& the cooks

& the single moms especially

& the weed dealers
& the teachers

& the meter maid who lets you slide

& the cab drivers who stop

& the nurse's swollen feet
& the braider's exhausted hands

2

        & the bartender
  & beyoncé
  & all her kids
        & the rabbi

  & the sad girls

      & the leather daddy who always stops to say *good morning*

& the boy crying on the train & the sudden abuela who rubs his back
& the uncle who offers him water & the drag queen who begins to hum

      o my presidents!
      my presidents!
      my presidents!
      my presidents!

    show me to our nation
my only border is my body

      i sing your names
      sing your names
      your names

       my mighty anthem

niggas!

love them two g's in the middle
hanging down like hands scooping
water from a river pinked by dusk. i love
how it starts in the nose (nig-) then
books it to the back of the mouth
& smacks the soft palate (-gas).
i love the smell of nigga on the tongue
& how it means that which is me
& them niggas over there too. it do my heart
well to think on niggas, lower my cholesterol
when i holler *NIGGAS!* when i walk
into a room & be nigga'd right back.
nigga every room i enter, i touch
the knob & nigga the door
into a door to an eternal eastside
hidden in the shea-slick hold of kin
& little bridges clasped black hands make
or how my nigga Josh place
his head against my head
& we each make our nigga a crown.
ain't that it? my niggas royal me
make me the whole damn castle
& me brick & me moat & i arrows
pointed at the distance ready
to ride for the two g's of my body
& the g's that made me
& the g's before
& the g's before.

how many of us have them?

friends! if i may interrupt right quick

i know y'all working, busy smoking & busy
trying to not, busy with the kids & moms

& busy with alone, but i have just seen
two boys—yes, black—on bikes—also black—
basketball shorts & they outside shoes, wild

laughing 'bout something i couldn't hear
over my own holler, trying to steady
the wheel & not hit they lil asses as they swerved
friend-drunk, making their little loops, sun-lotioned

faces screwed up with that first & cleanest love
we forget to name as such & hear me out
i'm not trying to diss lil dude, but in this golden hour
he kind of looked like Francine   off *Arthur*
same monkey mouth & all, ole *& i say HEY!* lookin'-ass boy

tho in a beautiful way, the best beautiful
same as i know all of us have looked
when wasted off love. o loves
y'all ugly asses have crowned me the worst names:
wayne brady, gay wiz khalifa, all kinds of bitches
& fags (tho only with *my* bitches & fags)

&, once, *the mark of Buddha* the year acne
scored my forehead with its bumpy faith.
o my niggas & my niggas who are not niggas
i been almost pissed myself, almost been boxin'
been tears & snot off your dozen wonders
been the giddy swine dancing the flame.
o my many hearts, y'all booty-faced

weird-ass ole-mojo-jojo-head asses
dusty chambers where my living dwells.
roast me! name me in the old ways, your shit talk
a river i wade, howling until it takes me.
i can't stop laughing, more river wades
down my throat. could be drowning
could be becoming the water, could be
a baptism from the inside out.

don't save me, i don't wanna be saved.
i been died laughing before, been seen
god's face & you have her teeth, my nig.
but   hers   ain't as yellow as   them   saffron shits
you   keep   stashed   in   your   gloryfoul mouth
my friend! my friends! my niggas! my wives!
i got a crush on each one of your dumb faces
smashing into my heart like idiot cardinals into glass
but i am a big-ass glass bird, a stupid monster

crashing through the window & becoming it
just to make you laugh. Andrew used to say
friendship is so friendship   & ain't it?
even after Andrew gave it on over to whatever
he was still my nigga. when they turned his body
to dust he was still my dusty-ass boy.
don't you hear it? the dust on the fan calls me
a bum, say my hairline looks like it's thinking
about retirement. the dust in the car says i look
like a chubby slave, says i look too drunk, takes

my keys, drives me home. the wind is tangled
with the dust of the dead homies, carrying us over
to them, giggling in the mirror. hear them. hear
your long-gone girl tease your hair on the bus. hear them
rollin' when you sweep the broom across the beaten floor.
i miss them. all the dead. how young. how silly
to miss what you will become. i apologize.
sometimes it just catches up in me. love

& ghost get caught up in us like wind & birds
trapped in a sheet just the same. & my friends
is some birds, is some chicken-head mofos

who i would legit stomp a nigga for, do you feel me?
when they buried my nigga i put on my Timbs
walked into that hot August tried to beat his name
out the dirt. i beat the earth like a nigga.
i threw hands at the earth like a punk muhfucka
& the ground chuckled, said *my nigga. what is you doing?!*
you can't hear the wind drunk off the kindred lent?
can you hear the great roll from way off like a big nigga
laughing in an alley? how your dead auntie laugh
when she see you still ain't grew into that big-ass head!
like your real friend laugh when you still the same ugly
as yesterday! same ugly as always! same ugly as his last life!

jumped!

there, on the ground like dirt or a bird
December froze & May thawed, blood

misted, crying for any mother, the boy
who called your mama a bitch bleeds

our love for you, his wings frozen & fighting
our gust of sneakers.

we storm him because we love you
& your mama has fed us & only us

is allowed to call her out her name
because we know her name, Phyllis,

& she bad & only we can say so
& when we bad she has permission

from our mamas to beat us like we hers.
we hers like you hers. you our boy.

we pool our punches into the boy
like quarters for a bag of flaming hots.

we make him look like a bag of flaming hots.
lord forgive me, but i don't regret it

& on the real all these summers later
i miss it. i wish a little bit to gather round

a man & stomp in the name of love
beat what he said about my next to blood

back into his gleeyellow mouth, to make
his mouth a sparkling smashed tomato.

really tho. Leland, you remember
how we beat ole boy? our middle

        school ritual, his thirty-second eternity.
later, i licked his blood off my Nikes

      & dreamed we were water lilies
holding the water down.

     //

they were around me like

            nigga1

         nigga2   nigga3

       nigga4   me   nigga5

        nigga6   nigga7

         nigga8

    but what could be safer
    than a circle of boys
    too afraid of killing you
    to kill you?

the fists that broke my ribs also wanted me to live.

        i praise each one true god
        for each foot that wasn't
        a sharp anything.

each hand laid upon me like a rude & starving prayer.

i had always wanted 8 niggas on me, but not like that.

              after a while i started to   like it?
                   i leaned into it   unblocked my face.

the bottoms of their shoes the sweet of a well-chewed eraser.
              i was their promise. their ink.

        you should have heard them laugh
        a language so delicious i cracked up cracked grin & all.

i didn't know
a thing about love
until those boys
walked away
so happy.
              my heart pouring from my nose.

saw a video of a gang of bees swarming a hornet who killed
their bee-homie so i called to say i love you

we are in their love

honey bitch
you kin me
so good i would
kill on sight
if you asked
gun knife or bite
a man down
to bloodnectar
i say i would
cut an anyone
for you & people
have the scars
to prove it
& that ain't
a fact only true
for this poem
love knows
where to hide
the body
love knows
the deepest
rivers & softest
earth love
murders first
justifies later
so i guess
white folks
do love niggas
to bits

we are in their love we are in their love we are in their love we are in their love we are in their love we are in their love we are in their love we are in their love we are in their love

we are in their love we are in their love we are in their love we are in their love we are in their love we are in their love we are in their love we are in their love we are in their love

we are in their love

fall poem

the leaves done done their annual shimmy.
now the streetlight with no soft green curtain
cuts a silver blade across my bed

& my body. i didn't want to start with leaves
even though i love how the trees turn the color of aunts
& soul-train-line to the ground each October. no one

wants to hear a poem about fall; much prefer the fallen
body, something easy to mourn, body cut out of the light
body lit up with bullets. see how easy it is to bring up bullets?

is it possible to ban guns? even from this poem?
i lie in the light, body split by light, room too bright for sleep
thinking of the leaf-colored bodies, their weekly fall

how their bodies look like mounds of a tree's shed skin
a child could jump into them & play for hours.
there i go, talking about our dead & if you don't think

they are your dead, i've run from your hands. they are red
like the tree down the street, a hot-air balloon
of blood, the leaves dyed fruit-punch red, red as a child's red mouth

after an afternoon spent on the porch with a bag of takis
watching other kids walk by, waiting for kids who don't
pass anymore on the other side of summer, who maybe go

to a different school or moved out east or made like a tree
& now sleep in a box made from one.

rose

we were kindergarten sweethearts. you asked me. i said yes. you were a white girl & not pretty. i liked the shape of your face. it looked like a ball with hair. you were red & puffy. we broke because we were five. it mattered until it didn't. how big a fact at six seven even nine. i treated you like poop. everyone treated you same. you were the girl with the puffy red face. you were mean. so we were mean. or we were so you. we were nine ten eleven. we were so small & evil. you & barbara sliverman wrapped a jump rope around my neck after i called you a puffy-faced something. when we learned the word bitch, we called you bitch. someone was always willing to remind you of your shit. we were shit, ugly & needed to direct attention everywhere else. girls fought you. said you got around. made you untouchable & easy. you screamed. i remember you always at the top of your lungs. you were kind to your friends. no one liked any of y'all. it was dangerous to be your friend. you were red & dated. your folks shit broke. you were a girl & everyone wanted you to know you were a white frog. if you wished we all watched the last of our water turn to feathers or prayed our children are born with teeth where eyes should be, your prayer was fair. you deserved to parade us through a city of grandmas, smacking our faces, beating us with belts & shoes & whistling branches, pinching ears. if you saw me & stabbed me in the foot i'd understand. we were so mean. i was the bastard fuck in the mob of bastard fucks. the easily swayed torch. o rose, saint of getting roasted in the hallway, warrior queen of the misfits, my love, how did you survive us? if this finds you if there is still a you to find if you know this is about you if you read poems if you take breath into & out of your lungs & find this in a book or in the blue aurora of your phone & this is you: at times i wake in the middle of the night & think
we killed that girl.

i'm going back to Minnesota where sadness makes sense

o California, don't you know the sun is only a god
if you learn to starve for her? i'm over the ocean

i stood at its lip, dressed in down, praying for snow.
i know i'm strange, too much light makes me nervous

at least in this land where the trees always bear green.
i know something that doesn't die can't be beautiful.

have you ever stood on a frozen lake, California?
the sun above you, the snow & stalled sea—a field of mirror

all demanding to be the sun, everything around you
is light & it's gorgeous & if you stay too long it will kill you.

it's so sad, you know? you're the only warm thing for miles
the only thing that can't shine.

the flower who bloomed thru the fence in grandmama's yard

flowers is niggas too
this here nigga grown
snug into a chokehold

to set him free
would mean to behead him
some would split a nigga neck

let him bleed out tucked behind ear
tupac of a flower
white picket clasping the throat

descendent of a self-picked field
almost miraculous & out of context
like niggas in Utah

grander for his quarantine
how white niggas looked at me sometimes
petaled nigga child special only because it is

divorced from the garden
hands plucking my weedish bouquet
we love niggas we love niggas not

prisoner of wood & accident
he leaned himself into meaning
trapped in observation

well-bloomed nigga
annual like the death of aunties
locked in & strangled pretty

nosey-ass flower peeking his head
in search of greener grass now stuck
in a guillotine refusing to guillotine

assimilated into barrier
black cop of a flower
shimmied into place & now

you can only leave here
dead, silly nigga, fences
are for fences you trespassed

& now you locked up
the fence wears you
like a single yellow hair

you wear the fence
like a little boy
in his mother's blue gown

drowns or wishes to
why are you here living flower
in a dead tree

why you running from
what still rooted where you started
who the ghost who haunt your dirt

do they slick around your feet
gray as worms do they make
your mind feel like wasps

did you stick your head out
just to breathe only to have
your head bloom bigger

than the window do i pluck
you now or let you wilt on
your own o my nigga

my nigga is death any easier
if you can call your
killer kin

in lieu of a poem, i'd like to say

apricots & brown teeth in browner mouths gnashing dates & a clementine's underflesh under yellow nail & dates like auntie heads & the first time someone dried mango there was God & grandma's Sunday-only song & how the plums are better as plums dammit & i was wrong & a June's worth of moons & the kiss stain of the berries & lord the prunes & the miracle of other people's lives & none of my business & our hands sticky & a good empty & please please pass the bowl around again & the question of dried or ripe & the sex of grapes & too many dates & us us us us us & varied are the feast but so same the sound of love gorged & the women in the Y hijab a lily in the water & all of us who come from people who signed with x's & yesterday made delicacy in the wrinkle of the fruit & at the end of my name begins the lot of us

dogs!

scooby doo was trying to tell us
something when every time that
monster mask got snatched off it
was a greedy white dude.

//

in '97 a black comic gets on stage
says, *you ever notice how white dogs
be like woof woof & black dogs be
like ruff ruff motherfuckaaaaa!!*

//

the dog upstairs won't shut up &
i've thought of ending his noisy
little life but i have to remember
he matters, he matters & if i did,
the brown girl upstairs would cry
forever.

//

dog (n.): a man's best friend. (see:
fetch, roll over, K-9, good boy, put
down.) ex. *my dog died, i had to do
it with my own hands.*

dawg (n.): a man's best friend. (see:
blunt rolled already, handshake,
my nigga, put me on) ex. *my dawg
died, he did it with his own hands.*

//

dogs in this house eat the same thing we do. we eat greens, they eat greens. fried bologna, neck bones leftovers.

. . . he died from the suga, the gout or whatever came for big mama came back for the dog.

//

everybody love lassie, but what about sounder?

//

possible rite of passage number 37: graduating from outrunning the block's dogs to outrunning the block's police.

//

i too been called boy & expected to come, heel.

//

what animorph did you want to be? i wanted to be the boy who turned into the bird limp in the dog's wet mouth, holding me toward his human saying, *i made this for you.*

//

the dog upstairs needs to stop
running his mouth talking plenty
shit i can hear him up there fool
don't think i understand he don't
know i got a bark too teeth too
thumbs & a terrible child's mind.

//

something about *Air Bud* felt . . .
the talented obedient beast, the
roar of the eggshell crowd.

//

dogs aren't racist but they can be
trained to be as can the water as
can the trees as can gravity as can
anything marked by a pale hand
& turned bloodgold, a bitter king's
magic touch.

//

i'm the kind of werewolf who
turns into a shih tzu. ruff ruff
motherfucka.

//

while grandmama spoke on the
clean blood of Jesus, i watched
the hounds in the mud hot for
anything warm & thought of
something better to worship.

//

i stand in the dark bathroom in my tightest shortest short shorts my vaselined legs the only things catching light. i say, *i'm a real bitch* three times, clap my hands above my head. nothing happens. i walk back into the club, put my hand on a man's chest & it's a paw.

//

the gay agenda made *CatDog* to offer your child's gender to their seven-headed god.

//

a dead dog is a hero, a dead lion is a hero, a cloned sheep is a miracle a dead child is a tragedy depending on the color, the nation, the occupation or non-occupation of the parents.

//

during the new moon, i switch from an –a to the traditional –er, i raid the farm, smash the melon patch, swallow chickens whole spit out the bones ground down to smoke, howl *Geee-zuss!* toward the sky's great nothing.

//

ruff ruff motherfuckaaaaa!!
ruff ruff motherfuckaaaaa!!
ruff ruff motherfuckaaaaa!!
ruff ruff motherfuckaaaaa!!
ruff ruff motherfuckaaaaa!!
ruff ruff motherfuckaaaaa!!
ruff ruff motherfuckaaaaa!!

//

dog bred to smell the coke. dog
bred to smell the bomb. dog bred
to smell the nigger hid beneath the
floorboards.

//

dude's dog won't leave the room,
won't let his lord out of his sight,
won't let his master disappear,
won't let himself go hungry, won't
let nothing happen to the one who
brings the water, even if it means
being owned, being witness to his
hunger or maybe he's just dumb.

//

stay. open. stay. look at me. stay.
open. teeth. bad. bad. stay. open.
treat. treat. pant. wag. treat. good.
stay. good. stay.

//

i listen to DMX smoking a blunt
doing bout 90 in a 55 when the
cop ask if i know why he pulled me
over i bark, *i'm just trying to be me.*

//

the dog upstairs won't shut up
but i can't hate him, he's up there
alone all day, making noise must
be the only way he knows he's not
a ghost.

ode to gold teeth

gold gate of grandpa's holler
midas touch his blue hum
honeymetal perfuming prayers

crowns who crowned his crowns
made even his vomit expensive
gangster grill before gangsta grillz

marked my granddaddy OG of the gin
sermon & front-porch pulpit
made everything he said sound gold-rimmed

bible or gold-rimmed tires
gangsta white walls, TV antennas
cross the back of your legs talk smart

even his punishments sparkled.
o his golds, when young i thought
your mustard gleam meant my papa

was a kind of hero, alien, or stone
so confused on how he hid
all those suns so near his tongue

his mouth held the day hostage
but didn't swallow it. o butter glow
country tiara, ghetto kingdom

of molars, glinting hallelujah
pork stuck near the black gums
forgive me, forgive me, citizens

of my papa's dead mouth
i stole you from behind his cold
flap at the funeral, i knew you were

not teeth, but seeds. forgive me
who planted you between the collards
& the hull peas, who waters you

daily with erk & jerk & prays for rain.
with enough belief a boy will sprout
with 24-karat skin, his whole

body one gold tooth, yellow
ballad, plaqued, unbreakable
& i will raise him right.

on faggotness

the word faggot. means different. any boy-shaped. child who behaves a way. someone else's tenderness. revolted toward the child. the first time i remember. being called that kind. mother's room. mother's mirror. mother's dress. spinning. some small song. grand. pa said. *that boy gonna be a. faggot.* i didn't. know what it meant. but it had to be. akin to king. or mighty. different. a good kind. but then i looked it up in his eyes. saw my body upside down.

    //

sitting on the ledge of. the tub holding down the lever so the water'll drain. watching a bit of black. grace toward the soft whirl & think. if the black bit was human sized it would be. flying. driving. drowning. being in the river when the river suddenly surges. half-tipsy & sixteen. summer-drunk. last day of camp. *mama pick me up.* grandma in backseat. ride home. she ask. how was it. i say. great. she ask. what happened. i say. a boy came out. & no one made a big deal. she ask. how that make you feel. i say. *good. cause i'm bi.* summer gone. dumb tongued. wasted pilot. whoa whoa whoa whoa. sweet Jesus. flagrant foul. mayday mayday. house turned ash due to sleep cigarette. accidental fag. standing in a puddle. suddenly the Mississippi. i was swept a great distance at a startling speed.

//

it's been awhile since. a body was inside my body. summer. & now i think how lonely. i am standing next to the oven for heat. so much depends on sex. once you have had it & had it well. only the little ruins follow. i am no stranger. many a man ruined me for both our pleasures. what recent history calls a faggot. what the Greeks called Greek. what some needed no language for. faggot at the moment. i'm always talking. with sam & cam & paula & hieu. my faggots. what makes a fag a fag. one theory rings true. it's not the sex. the being filled. but the emptiness. void you didn't know was. until someone stopped it up. a particular strangeness. i was a faggot in first grade. full of so little. one day in the car heading somewhere. probably the park. my friend Alex asked my mom where my father was. never occurred to me. i didn't have a father. when my friend Ben came over to play all i had was barbies. & he asked whose they were. my cousin's. my girl cousin's. i hadn't a cousin to speak of. i knew to hide. the void. void a more boyish & fathered thing should occupy. plenty straight man faggots too. nothing to do. with what a boy wants. another boy to do to him. everything to do. with how we speak of the silver miles & miles we know. in us. pulsing gray. hungry to be. the land.

//

particular walk. particular wrist. particular speech. particular clothes. particular piercings. particular knowledge. particular ways of eating particular things. particular sounds. particular swallow. particular motions. particular honey. particular eyes. particular fear. particular holler. particular curve. particular midnights. particular shame. particular milk. particular beast. particular cage. particular freedoms. particular blocks. particular glances. particular running. particular gods. particular beliefs. particular hells. particular economies. particular arrangements. particular secrets. particular shade. particular bliss. particular deeds. particular punishments. particular lonely. particular grief.

//

i try not to see myself. in the broken humidifier. nor the molded potato. the freezer-burned chuck roast. woke up with my mind. steady on the old women at the gym in corduroys. what roads have led them to treadmills. i want to say. they are faggots. i want to claim their strange. particular it is. their well-ironed gym clothes. the women. some in t-shirts. most in sweaters. shiny foreheads & creased pants. cycling thru the body. stopping for water. stopping to chat with Barb. fearing the knees. working the shoulders. stopping to pee. braving the knees. begging their machine. to master the machine. bad joints & all. i love them. my corduroy coven. little nana faggots. i see it. in them. they know time. is not a river. not quite. like a lover. but a thing that leaves you. until it's gone.

self-portrait as '90s R&B video

lately i've been opening doors in slow motion
& find myself wearing loose white silks
in rooms packed with wind machines & dusk.

i have a tendency to be sad near windows
thinking of all the problems i have
with my man with his triflin yellow ass.

my man is more a concept than anything.
at dinner i watch red-pepper soup spill
onto his powder-blue button-down

& ask, *why don't you love me anymore?*
i sit on the couch with a wine glass full
of milk, cry in ways that frame me gorgeous

& fuckable. my girls come over & we light
his suits to spark our spliffs. my best bitch
tells me i need to get over him, say he don't

even exist, but what she know? i have all this
house to walk through, all these gowns to cry
on, all these windows to watch the rain.

there must be a man in this house who loves me
too much to do it well. there's a room
in my basement filled with water & gold & that's it.

water up to my well-managed waist
gold-link chains curl around my ankles
like a boa constrictor or the hands of a man

around a neck he once loved to bite.
i dip my head in, let even my hair get wet
& rise out the water Hood Venus

Afrodite, ghetto god with iced-out ropes draped
from my head & arms, covering my nipples
& ill nana just so. i could be a trophy for some

award show only niggas know, every rapper's
favorite ex, 1996 given a body & he don't
want this? i walk into my foyer cause i have

a foyer & say *who is she, nigga?* i promise
the hydrangeas flinch. my man is so fake
he don't exist. my girls was right—the suits

we lit were mine, my man is all in my head
& it's a bad head. tomorrow, after i run
& spend some time studying the mirror

i'll burn this whole shit down
like Left Eye would, like any good wife.
whatever survives will be my kingdom.

i hope i make it.

my bitch!

o bitch. my good bitch. bitch my heart.
dream bitch. bitch my salve. bitch my order.
bitch my willowed stream. bitch my legend.
bitch like a door. your name means *open*
in the language of my getting by. bitch sesame.
lets get together & paint our faces the color
of our mothers if our mothers were sad men
only soft in bad lights. let's swirl the deep grape
& coffee pencils until we look like odd planets
on our way to looking like the daughters
we secretly were. caked & cakes hairy
just short of grace. we look terrible
when we're the most beautiful girls in the world.
bitch my world. bitch my brother. bitch my rich trust.
i'll miss you most when they kill us.

sometimes i wish i felt the side effects

but there is no proof but proof
no mark but the good news

there is no bad news yet. again.
i wish i knew the nausea, its thick yell

in the morning, pregnant proof
that in you, life swells. i know

i'm not a mother, but i know what it is
to nurse a thing you want to kill

& can't. you learn to love it. yes.
i love my sweet virus. it is my proof

of life, my toxic angel, wasted utopia
what makes my blood my blood.

i get it now, how beauty so loved
her warden. you stare at fangs

long enough, even fangs pink
with your own blood look soft.

      //

low key, later, it felt like i got it
out the way, to finally know it

up close, see it in the mirror.
it doesn't feel good to say.

it doesn't feel good to know
your need outweighed your fear.

i braved the stupidest ocean. a man.
i waded in his stupid waters.

i took his stupid salt & let it
brine my skin, took his stupid

fish into my stupid hands & bit into it
like a stupid flapping plum. i kissed at

his stupid coral & stupid algae.
it was stupid. silly really. i knew nothing

that easy to get & good to feel
isn't also trying to eat you.

       //

knew what could happen. needed
no snake. grew the fruit myself.

was the vine & the rain & the light.
the dirt was me. the hands drilling

into the dirt were my hands.
i made the blade that cut me down.

but i only knew how to live
when i knew how i'll die.

i want to live. think i mean it.
took the pill even on the days

i thought i wouldn't survive myself.
gave my body a shot. love myself

at least that much. thank you, me.
thank you, genvoya, my seafoam savior.

thank you, sick blood, first husband, bff
dead river bright with salmon.

say it with your whole black mouth

say it with your whole black mouth: i am innocent.
& if you are not innocent, say this: i am worthy

of forgiveness, of breath after breath.
i tell you this: i let blue eyes dress me in guilt

walked around stores convinced the very skin
of my palm was stolen. what good has it brought?

days filled flinching thinking the sirens
were reaching for me. & when the sirens were mine

did i not make peace with God?
so many white people are alive

because we know how to control ourselves.
how many times have we died on a whim

wielded like gallows in their sun-shy hands?
here, standing in my own body, i say: next time

they murder us for the crime of their imaginations
i don't know what i'll do.

i did not come to preach of peace
for that's not the hunted's duty.

i came here to say what i can't say
without my name being added to a list

what my mother fears i will say
what she wishes to say herself

i came here to say

                        i can't bring myself to write it down

sometimes i dream of pulling an apology
from a pig's collared neck & wake up crackin' up

if i dream of setting fire to cul-de-sacs
i wake chained to the bed

i don't like thinking about doing to white folks
what white folks done to us

when i do

            can't say

        i don't dance

o my people

        how long will we

reach for God

        instead of something

        sharper?

shout out to my niggas in Mexico

it's true! we made beyond do with what the ships left
in our mouths. it's true! our histories stink
of interruption, our long stories impossible

to tell for real without their names
which became our names. all that plot
twisted up in the blood, but tonight the land hums

all our dead's beautiful bones, so let's have a party!
bring your niggas! i'll bring mine. what else
do we share, cousin? drums & cornmeal?

our mothers make the same face when
they think of God, their dead sisters, the rent.
shout out to all your mothers! shout out

to all my Mexican niggas. we need a bigger table now.
let's get some food going. get the tias & aunties
still alive up here. let us wash their feet this time

before they stand against the hours despite the knees
& the water there to knead & batter & cuss the slow rice
so everybody can be a little less hungry. shout out

all the aunties. do you think God knows the white men
who leash the land hate aunties?
what do the approved uncles have to say?

there's already so much to deal with amongst our own
folks to worry their white shit falling like rejected prayers.
ugh! i didn't want to talk about them today.

let's start over. would you like some greens?
do you fuck with Patti LaBelle? Rubén Blades?
Panameño cat? nice with it. we'll listen to him next.

shout out my niggas in Panama. some more chairs now.
& all the Jamaican niggas now native to Colón, what up?
& the Caribbean niggas who didn't already come

when i said come, come on now. all my African niggas
if y'all ain't already here, get here. & the rest
of the niggas in this place they called the Americas, come on!

come on all my niggas who still call this land its older names.
& my Asian niggas, y'all already know. bring the broth
your auntie makes when she wants to make your mama look bad.

hurry on, y'all! we got so much kicking it to do!
i see some slow-moving Arab cats over there!
& some slow Muslim niggas too! didn't you hear me

say y'all names? come! if you must fly in from your island
bring the island with! bring your cousins, your wine, your rituals as gifts!
all y'all come quick! i'm sorry to use whole damn continents

& shit to sum up the diasporas within our diasporas
i'm just trying to get the word out! we got a jam going!
bring ya folks! bring whatever your mama considers gospel.

not the text, but the feeling. tell me what song is likely on
when our mother finds herself on the floor, weeping
beckoning whoever lurks behind the sky.

we'll play that loud. look! our fathers have found each other
in each other, they're over yonder teaching each other
what they know to do with dominos, trading curse words

like fourth graders with too much language & no supervision.
we got time! this could go for a moon or two! they said the fish
is gonna take until tomorrow. the lamb longer. the rice is ready tho.

we got some more chairs in the basement. upstairs a room
for crying. a room for prayer. somebody girlfriend
doing tarot over there. look at our nieces jumping into stars!

come on niggas! is there a nigga in Antarctica? her too!
any place where they came & handed out new names
come. come on, niggas! i know the word is complicated

but it's my favorite word! we'll talk about it later.
& yes. yes, it's intentional.
                              they were never invited.

white niggas

your narrative & my narrative go behind the house
& just have it out for once. one lunges with a shiv

the lunged-at pulls it into place. they know the choreo
of this marriage, their good-time war. i understand

the shape of it: we don't read the same articles, don't
consider the same things knowledge, don't believe in

the same god in the same way. i get it. we know little
similar, sure, the joy of a good piss, the smell

of fresh-cut lemon, the feeling of making it home
alive. now, if i am trying to avoid you to stay alive

& you are trying to avoid me to stay alive, what is that
the definition of? all this blood & still no truce.

my adopted twin, we've been at it for years
you run around scared of the idea of me, i run away

from your actual you with your actual instruments
of my end: badge, bullet, post, gas, rope, opinion.

you have murdered me for centuries & still i fix
my mouth to say love is possible. it is. it is? if you

come to my door thirsty, i'll turn the faucet & fill
the glass. if i come to your stoop, don't shoot.

what was said at the bus stop

lately has been a long time
says the girl from Pakistan, Lahore to be specific
at the bus stop when the white man
ask her where she's from & then
says *oh, you from Lahore?*
it's pretty bad over there lately.

lately has been a long time
she says & we look at each other & the look says
yes, i too wish dude would stop
asking us about where we from
but on the other side of our side eyes
is maybe a hand where hands do no good
a look to say, *yes, i know lately has been*
a long time for your people too
& i'm sorry the world is so good at making
us feel like we have to fight for space
to fight for our lives

"solidarity" is a word, a lot of people say it
i'm not sure what it means in the flesh
i know i love & have cried for my friends
their browns a different brown than mine
i've danced their dances when taught
& tasted how their mothers miracle the rice
different than mine. i know sometimes
i can't see beyond my own pain, past black
& white, how bullets love any flesh.
i know it's foolish to compare.
what advice do the drowned have for the burned?
what gossip is there between the hanged & the buried?

& i want to reach across our great distance
that is sometimes an ocean & sometimes centimeters
& say, *look. your people, my people, all that has happened*
to us & still make love under rusted moons, still pull

children from the mothers & name them
still teach them to dance & your pain is not mine
& is no less & is mine & i pray to my god your god
blesses you with mercy & i have tasted your food & understand
how it is a good home & i don't know your language
but i understand your songs & i cried when they came
for your uncles & when you buried your niece
i wanted the world to burn in the child's brief memory
& still, still, still, still, still, still, still, still, still
& i have stood by you in the soft shawl of morning
waiting & breathing & waiting

i didn't like you when i met you

but like the funk of a dude unwashed & sun-whooped
i learned the need. & like dude, you were stank & i
was stank right back, two skunks pissed & pissing, smelling like skunks.
but somehow (was it mutual hate for a stanker fuck? a song
our dueling shoulders found each other in? a synced nod?
being the only of our kind in a room full of not-us?) here we live
two stank bitches, thick as mothers, a lil gone off love's gold milk.
i didn't know when i thought, *i don't like that hoe*, it was just
my reflection i couldn't stand. i saw it. the way you would break me
into a better me. i ran from it. like any child, i saw my medicine
& it looked so sharp, so exact, a blade fit to the curve of my name.
what a shame. i was slow to you. walked up on you like a bee trapped
in a car—all that fear pent in my wings, those screaming, swatting giants
& then, finally, the window, the wind, the flowers, the hive
myqueenmyqueenmyqueen!

for Andrew

    i. swagged-out Jesus

named yourself that mess when you wore the rainbow

beaded crown à la Stevie in the '70s & let the great religion

of your belly hang like some Southside Buddha

with a boombox dangling from your neck old Radio

Raheem looking ass dude walking around blasting Ye

random folk following you like you were the Christ

of the night or maybe just a mirage of bass

& flesh stained with June's turmeric—

o if the gods would let me edit & loop

o if i could stop here—

ii. ending with nothing

~~what do you do when a boy lynches himself~~
          ~~when the mob isn't after his skin~~

~~but under it, when anything that can hold~~
          ~~his weight becomes a tree, when you can't~~

~~close your eyes & not see him there—~~
          ~~low planet, swayed orbit~~

~~cooling rapidly?~~ i counted the things
          used to end a boy but forgot

the boy himself. how could i?
          i considered it

the matter of you neither created
          nor destroyed but something

we have no word for, only myth
          & faith & doubt about the place

that lives—we hope lives—after the body
          spits out the soul like a seed.

we are left to harvest this black fruit—
          your name perched in past tense.

what good is hiding the gun
          & locking the cabinet if the boy

can still find his own hands?
          if anything that loops can be a rope?

i want to believe you did an Ebo thing
          soaring the ocean floor to an older home

but dammit, Andrew
        they turned you into dust. dust.

your whole body gray in a brass bowl
        waiting to be scattered, to jewel

the wind, get caught in our eyes.
        in dreams, i pull at a rope for hours

miles of rope & rope & my bloody
        hands & when i get to the end—

you, hooked & laughing
        so hard i wake up to the windows

rattling with no storm or breeze
        or world out there at all.

iii. for the dead homie

bury me under your heft of titles:
love who makes me rude to other loves
love who makes me like me like me
rose sweet chemical in the blood
tender wind that makes the brain blush
storm that scares the storm away.
in me—a monument to your fray.
in you—a trap door back to myself.
before holy there was your grace
messiah of the random Wednesday.
a world without you is not a world.
thy terrain & bounty include my hands.
my main. higher light in a room of light.
when you went i choked the dirt.

//

when you went i choked on dirt
i ate my way to Australia, i smoked hella
i dressed in headlights & sirens
i thought about it, i put the pills back
i burned the medicine cabinet, burned
the house, burned the city, burned
the last years down to cinders & drank
yes i drank them down, i wanted to be
bloated with fact: you are not
a thing i can touch, a voice i can call
a shot at the bar, a shot at making it big
but didn't you? didn't you make it big, fam?
aren't you all of it now? i call for God.
i call for God but out comes your name.

//

i call for God & out comes your name
& then your blood next, wraps its weight
around your christening. next, bone-
colored seeds plant themselves in you
& become bones, bloom fields of muscle
& organs from orchids, little dandelions
that dry into skin. next come seeds
for your eyes, a seed for your voice
a seed to makes you dance, a seed
that looks like your mother & a boy
comes flying right out my mouth
burrows root & prayer into your chest
& had he always been there? the boy
beautiful & waiting for someone to see?

     //

beautiful & waiting by some sea
purple with the waves of your laugh
your frequency somewhere between
sound & light, bright note singeing dawn.
to arrive to you would be heaven enough.
somewhere, you're a city with a boy
in every window calling down to me.
i call back. our voices fat the air
with nectarines. you laugh so hard
you become the wind & every ribbon it holds.
your body is all silk & all air, you are in my hair.
you're an opal braid, an amethyst twist.
give me that eternity—i'll breathe
you in, you nourish & strangle.

     //

i breathe you. in you, i nourish. strangle
your name out my mouth if you could
but you are a smoke i can swallow, fire
rich with something thicker, honey begat
by flames, the wet of burned skin.
your name is honeydew glass. i hunger
& bleed for it, cough up burgundy mercies
for it, but it's always true the same way.
my nigga is gone. he took himself away
from himself, he flung himself higher
than the oldest light i know, light so old
it's gone from where it started & is seen
only years from here. it's true, a star
withers here, blooms up in a farther sky.

//

"withers here, blooms up in a farther sky."
pretty right? but wasn't shit cute.
i was ugly with your going. i had its bad teeth
& scabs, heaving up dark, my skin clotting
then becoming like black tumbleweeds.
i was a hollow block, a ghost hood
where liquor tips itself sideways
bleeds out in memory of hands.
over the toilet, nothing left to leave me
but sound. i was not ready to be your witness
i broke like champagne against your vessel.
but to see your mother, to see her see you
settled into a jar? what's it like to lose all that?
your child? your ark? your lil friend? your summer?

//

your fat cheeks, your ark arms, your summer
everything, your royal radius, your bleeding yes
the verb your name makes, so much
to smile about in spite of that final data.
in your honor, we plant an acre of blue
a row of collards for you to bouquet or boil
we sing a hymn made of chamomile & kush
sing our lines of sparks & gone suns
until our song is a wall of light so thin
you could miss it so wide it halves the world
& out the bright, you stumble
pat yourself gently &

enough.

1989–2016

that close. edge of

almost. fled. looked

dead. was. tried. kept

it up. kept my

mouth so close. pills

nearer. seer

said. dust dust. was.

then wasn't. missed.

hole in a night.

that was my face.

almost followed.

river's no. won't

mirror. it was

summer. November

so quick. i rocked

all gray. nickel

& sky. my

last winter. just

past my touch. axed

my arms. i wrote

with aim. the year came.

depression food

roma™ brand frozen pizzas—pepperoni—3 for 10

plums 5 hours before mush

nacho cheese doritos + whatever cheese is left + 45 seconds on high

bootleg frosted flakes by the fist

yogurt month past best by so more yogurter i guess

endless wendy's

instant coffee + hard honey

& dark. bitch, i gagged.

gnarled night, my fucked grill

i gnash double mint & nina while he pipes me up

when nutted, his swisher sweet fingers spoon

what i rocket back in as feed, i pig

sure, i wanted to be stuffed

by what i gave away gladly

it's just cum, i say his name

as he empties inside my empty

gasping like thawed tilapia

undetectable

soundless, it crosses a line, quiets into a seed

& then whatever makes a seed. almost like gone

but not gone. the air kept its shape. not antimatter

but the memory of matter. or of it mattering. it doesn't

cross my mind now that it whispers so soft it's almost

silence. but it's not. someone dragged the screaming boy

so deep into the woods he sounds like the trees now.

gone enough. almost never here. daily, swallowed

within a certain window, a pale green trail on the tongue

the pale green pill makes before it's divvied among

the ghettos of blood, dissolves & absolves

my scarlet brand, ritual & proof. surely science

& witchcraft have the same face. my mother

praises God for this & surely it is his face too.

regimen, you are my miracle. this swallowing

my muscular cult. i am not faithful to much.

i am less a genius of worship than i let on.

but the pill, emerald dialect singing the malady

away. not away. far enough. for now.

i am the most important species in my body.

but one dead boy makes the whole forest

a grave. & he's in there, in me, in the middle

of all that green. you probably thought

he was fruit.

all the good dick lives in Brooklyn Park

& where do they keep the good shit in your town?
that fair-trade nana, them gushy gushy schools?
when i roll up on dude house & ain't seen

no grocery store in miles & there's
a liquor store next to a liquor store next to
a little caesars i know the dick gon be bomb.

there's a stereotype there—mandingo myth
slave quarter bathhouse, animal animal
experiencing need & so down for whatever.

that project dick. section 8 inches. pipe
make you call the super. when in the moment
i like to tell a nigga to fuck me like a loan.

may all the hood niggas who humor my wet
be blessed with some fly shit: 24s, condos
enough & some healthcare. i swear

buddy who rocks me best gets thinner by the day.
he can't afford the pills that keep me round & blood quiet.
i told him they got programs for prescription assistance

doctors, all kinds of help, but that would
mean to admit what we try so hard to forget.
my poor god. all kinds of broke a body can be.

i kiss him with the pill coming apart on my tongue.
i hope it's enough to fill both of us out. we split it
like gas, like the brown blunt's brown guts.

broke n rice

wit h bee f a nd veg gi es
b less ed wi th an e gg
sa ff ro n sul li ed c hil lin
w ith g arl ic or d irty n ot qu ite
re d bu ggin the bea ns
or jus t ri ce, wat er th e mi ra cl e
of sa lt t he gr a in s pr omi se
to pil lo w an d st retc h
i u sed to ha te r i ce
hat ed it   h ated h ow
br oke it sou nde d
rice rice rice a po cket
w ith thr ee co p per co ins
hu n ger s tamb our ine
i h ate d al l of it
h ated the w ate r
gh ostbl eac hed by sta rc h
hat ed th e p uff y mo on s
po ckin g my sto m a ch
lik e a si ck ne ss
end in g sic kn ess
hat ed ev eryth ing
th at i woul d mar ry no w
          l eg it wo uld
i wo uld m a rry wa ter
coul d it hav e me
wi tho ut de adi ng me
i d m arry the m oon
cha nge my n ame
to it s ho ur
i wou ld w ed t he y o lk
go ld r ice stu ck
in th e yo lk yell ow tee th
of m y hom e girls w ere it n ot
alr eady jew els
mini ng th eir lau ghs

bl in ge d ou t li ke a do w ry
           shi ning
nex t to th e bi lls of m int
       bov ine rib bons
           co n fet t ied c ar rots

C.R.E.A.M.
after Wu-Tang, after Morgan Parker

in the morning i think about money

green horned lord of my waking

forest in which i stumbled toward no salvation

prison of emerald & pennies

in my wallet i keep anxiety & a condom

i used to sell my body but now my blood spoiled

all my favorite songs warn me to get money

i'd rob a bank but i'm a poet

i'm so broke i'm a genius

if i was white, i'd take pictures of other pictures & sell them for six figures (happened)

i come from sharecroppers who come from slaves who do not come from kings

sometimes i pay the weed man before i pay the light bill

sometimes is a synonym for often

i just want a rich white sugar daddy & i'll be straight

i feel most colored when i'm looking at my bank account

when i scream *ball so hard motherfuckas wanna find me*

sally may a motherfucka

i spent one summer stealing from three different ragstocks

always bought a ring

if i went to jail i'd live rent free but there is no way to avoid making white people richer

a prison is a plantation made of stone & steel

being locked up for selling drugs = being locked up for trying to feed your loves

i used to help him bag it up

a bald fade cost 20 bones nowadays

my grandmama is great at saving money

what's a blacker tax than blackness?

before my grandfather passed he showed me where he hid his money & his gun

what cost more than being poor?

my aunt can't hold on to a dollar, a job, her mind

how much the power ball this week?

imma print my own money & be my own god & live forever in a green frame

i was warm within my mother's broke

don't ask me about my taxes

the b in debt is a silent black trapped

old confession & new

sounds crazy, but it feels like truth. i'll tell you again.
maybe i practiced for it, auditioned even, applied.
what the doctor told me was not news, was legend
catching up to me, a blood whispering
you were born for this. i tell you—i was not shocked
but confirmed. enlisted? i am on the battlefield
& i am the field & the battle & the casualty & the gun.
my war is but a rumor & is not war. at the end of me
there is a boy i barely remember, barely ever knew
saying, *don't worry, don't worry, don't worry, don't worry.*

so now that it's an old fact, can it be useful?
that which hasn't killed you yet can pay the rent
if you play it right. keep it really real
many niggas gettin' paid off the cruelty
of whites, why not make the blood
a business? take it. here's what happened to me.
while you marvel at it imma run to the store.
my blood brings me closer to death
talking about it has bought me new boots
a summer's worth of car notes, organic everything.

gay cancer

Melvin, Assanto, Essex, my Saint
Laurent, Xtravaganza   House of
    sissy & boosted silk   dirt throned
with your too soon   it grew
            in me too   blood's gossip
cum cussed   gifted to us
      from us   yes   it grows by the day
still   i'm sorry   we are still in the midst
of ourselves   here   a pill for your grave
      a door to our later years
you deserved   o mother   o sweet unc
   who we miss & never knew
                        is that you?
   my wrist to my ear
                you're here

happy hour

grandma say she going to the funeral to see who all there
like i say i'm 'bout to grab a drink. the woman, not someone
she knew too well, but someone of a similar age & blackness
southern daughter spun north out of promise or terror-

toned night, who fled into winter to escape the pale rope-
skinned good ole boys just being boys, but that's not on her
mind right now, *just help me get this necklace on* she say
& i latch the gold around her, my grandma a night

sky of moles on her face, dark stars glowing in the honey
a mole per friend, per friend of friend who now feeds the worms
& speaks to her thru the swell of tomatoes, the exact yellow
of the tulips in the garden, each bloom a gonelove saying hello

just stopping by for a summer & then, again, come winter, they go
to the funeral early & count the living, grandma & her girl Mary
headed to gather a body like i sometimes call my play-kin
to pass a bottle of hen—Mary, whose blacker hair my grandma

has surely held back on a sour friday, who she calls
sometimes with nothing to say, just to sit on the phone
& be alive together for a while, now in the diamond years
of friendship, after the children have been born & born their own

& some of them have died & the husbands have gone first
& another friend & another friend & an old love & a last
as the world throttles into what was once imaginary
waiting for a God they've believed in for decades to show

her face, surely their own faces & hopefully before they find themselves
raising a glass in a room of empty glasses, sipping whiskey
                no, not whiskey, a glass wet with browner ghost.

drink your dead. get throwed off their leaving. the duty of the last.

waiting on you to die so i can be myself

a thousand years of daughters, then me.
what else could i have learned to be?

girl after girl after giving herself to herself
one long ring-shout name, monarchy of copper

& coal shoulders. the body too is a garment.
i learn this best from the snake angulating

out of her pork-rind dress. i crawl out of myself
into myself, take refuge where i flee.

once, i snatched my heart out like a track
& found not a heart, but two girls forever

playing slide on a porch in my chest.
who knows how they keep count

they could be a single girl doubled
& joined at the hands. i'm stalling.

i want to say something without saying it
but there's no time. i'm waiting for a few folks

i love dearly to die so i can be myself.
please don't make me say who.

bitch, the garments i'd buy if my baby
wasn't alive. if they woke up at their wake

they might not recognize that woman
in the front making all that noise.

the fat one with the switch

stare so long they gotta growl

faggot to justify it. f-sounds

an excuse to bite they lips

the t-word just to taste.

dicks hard as consonants in dickies.

question-mark thick, you fuck they head up.

damn any desire that sneaks you into laundry rooms

& strikes you in the street out of fear of itself.

they disrupt themselves with your body

& call it your fault, bury you in night

but dark is cheap dirt. temporary earth.

with the sun comes the news of you.

     another.

          another.

i wanted to write an ode. it still could be.

but first, some silence for the girls

hurried into after 'cause some dude

felt his blood rush on sight

& it was the first time he knew he had blood.

not even the razor taught him that

not his daughter's birth

not his clotted mammy

not Christ. just like a man.

he saw God

& instinct told him *kill it*.

my poems

my poems are fed up & getting violent.

i whisper to them *tender tender bridge bridge* but they say *bitch ain't no time, make me a weapon!*

i hold a poem to a judge's neck until he's not a judge anymore.

i tuck a poem next to my dick, sneak it on the plane.

a poem goes off in the capitol, i raise a glass in unison.

i mail a poem to 3/4ths of the senate, they choke off the scent.

my mentor said once a poem can be whatever you want it to be.

so i bury the poem in the river & the body in the fire.

i poem a nazi i went to college with in the jaw until his face hangs a bone tambourine.

i poem ten police a day.

i poem the mayor with my bare hands.

i poem the hands off the men who did what they know they did.

i poem a racist woman into a whistle & feel only a little bad.

i poem the president on live TV, his head raised above my head, i say *Baldwin said.*

i call my loves & ask for their lists.

i poem them all. i poem them all with a grin, bitch.

poemed in the chair, handless, volts ready to run me, when they ask me what i regret

i poem *multitudes multitudes multitudes.*

trees!

y'all! they look like slow green explosions!

thick as the best fro in the clique!

a clique of them! a whole hood of soft jade!

stadium of limes how they look

gathered at the roots & at the leaves!

i'm a little beside myself, driving thru Mississippi

with tish, who is indeed a part of myself. she say

i wish i could take a picture of all this green

but it's raining so we can't step out to photograph

these perfect emerald lungs, these giant, ancient niggas.

they must be niggas, right? how brown & giving they are.

their fruit cousin to our hands, their flowers our songs.

i wonder if i went a year without lotion

if my skin would dry into bark & naps would drink

the day as my toes kinked with thirst?

do you think that's how trees were invented?

a bunch of niggas stood still in a field waiting

for a sign from older gods, their breath a prayer

until breath was their only action. if i could

be a tree, i'd know God is real. if i could be

a tree, there'd be a heart knifed into me

that'd read *i ♡ all my niggas!*

if i could stand still in a field with tish & blaire

& josh & jamila & cam & aaron & nate

& angel & morgan & britteney & kelsey &

krysta & d'allen & kamia & dorian & thiahera

& nabila & safia & cortney & jayson & phillip

& lamar & hanif & eve & chris & dom & saeed

& brandon & amber & adora & britney & chinaka

& james & leland & devray & deangelo

& all the niggas whose names burst my heart

to joyful smithereens with their bright seeds

i would be the happiest tree

i'd let the birds live in me

glad to breathe in my constellation of green

budding stars. o my god of negros

& foliage, roots & roots & roots, here we are

black & ashy & filtering air, ready

to be the forest, deliver us into an axeless world!

sweet mother of chlorophyll & melanin!

branch & braid! dogwood & all my dawgs!

we stand, waiting to be made evergreen!

we see your promise in the noonstar!

hear your word in the rain!

my nig

this ain't about language
but who language holds

those niggas who say my name
like it's good news. i'm in love

with purple gums, the yellow stain
of front teeth, the bit of plaque

unbrushed away revealed when
my niggas laugh. o loves

i know God is for i have seen you
throw language in the air

& watched the clouds turn heavy
bronze, i have seen tears well

in the corners of your eyes
when you are overcome

& that little wet is all
the sea i need.

we are alive & amen
someone of us are dead

but they are alive in language amen
heaven be your blunted breath

your chapped & sharp shade
your ashy elbows & lotion prayers.

i need no church but my niggas' arms
i need no savior but their love

oh sweet God if you be my nigga
don't never take my niggas from me

lest i be a black & yolkless language
lest i be tabernacle at the bottom

of the sea, lest i be whittled down
to not a nigga but a n-word

one letter to say a thing about shame
keep me free from that language.

let me live on the tongues
of my people & when they gone

from this world then i have no use
for me, let language end when they end

let my breath jump off the cliff
with them, let me be a follower

into a greater world, where streets
are paved with our enemies' teeth

& the angels sing of shine
where the rivers flow milk & honey

& hennessey & kool-aid &
none of that, just give me

the heaven of now, just give me
days near water with my niggas.

just leave me be in sun
surrounded by my nigs

as we get blacker
we caramelized children

of dark stars, we summer
kin, august colored, my brick

colored friends, the safety
that is them being, the peace

i feel when near their hands
when they press green

in paper & seal with their lips
piff kiss, hosanna the rope

a text message be
for how many

times was i saved by the ding
of *hey, how you?* or *what you*

on, hoe? hallelujah the boat
of being bored with homies

the heaven of my niggas
in a silent room.

holy my darkest hours the only
thing that kept the blade

from my wrist & closed
the medicine cabinet was

the thought of my friends
in a room dressed in black

& browns not their skin, how
could i do that to them?

how could i deny us
the grace of accidents

& old age, the laws of
disease & holy sick?

there is already so much
trying to end us so let

it not include our hands
today, let us not be dead

& red-handed for it
not today, not never

not yet.

notes

dear suicide

>how is the war? is it eating?
>tell me of girls charging
>backward into dumb tides
>death's wet mouth lapping
>their ankles, knees, eyebrows.
>tell me of sissies drunk
>fireworks rocketing into earth
>angels etched in cement.
>how is the war? does it have
>a wife? does she know how
>the bodies got in her bed?

dear suicide

>i know your real name.
>i bind you from doing harm.
>i enter the room like a germ.
>i say your name, it is my name.
>the walls cave around me like a good aunt.
>the window hums. the door rocks me.
>the dresser leaves to go make tea.
>the room knows my name.
>it binds us from doing harm.

dear suicide

>where are you keeping my friends?
>every cup i turn over holds only air.
>i jimmy open a tulip expecting their faces
>but find only the yellow heart.
>what have you done with them?
>yesterday i took my body off
>beat it on the front steps with a broom
>& not one of them

came giggling out my skin
yelling *you found me!*
not one of them i called for
was already in my hand.

dear suicide

you a mutual friend
a wedding guest, a kind
of mother, a kind of self
love, a kind of freedom.
i wish you were a myth
but mothers my color
have picked ocean
over boat have sent
children to school
in rivers. i known niggas
who just needed
quiet. i seen you
dance, it made me hard.
i would not deny you
what others have found
in the sweet mildew
behind your ear. i know
what happens when you
ask for a kiss, it's all
tongue, you don't
unlatch, you suck
face until the body
is gone.

dear suicide

that one? i promised him
i would kill for him
& my nigga was my nigga
& my word is my word.
dear suicide, where are you?

come see me. come outside.
i am at your door, suicide.
i'll wait. i've offed my earrings
& vaselined my face. i put on
my good sweats for this.
i brought no weapon but my fist.

dear suicide

you made my kin thin air.
his entire body dead as hair.
you said his name like a dare.
you've done your share.
i ride down lake street friendbare
to lake of isles, wet pairs
stare back & we compare
our mirror glares. fish scare
into outlines, i blare
a moon's wanting, i wear
their faces on t-shirts, little flares
in case i bootleg my own prayer
& submit to your dark affair.
tell me they're in your care.
                    be fair.
heaven or hell, i hope my niggas' all there
if i ever use the air as a stair.

acknowledgments

you save me half a bag of skins, the hard parts, my fav, dusted orange with hot

O

you say we can't go to the bar cause you're taking your braids out

i come over, we watch madea while we pull you from you

O

you make us tacos with the shells i like & you don't

O

i get too drunk at the party, you scoop my pizza from the sink with a solo cup,
all that red

O

you, in the morning, bong water grin, wet chin

O

you, in the lawless dark, laughing like a room of women laugh

at a man who thinks his knowledge is knowledge

O

i text you & you say, *i was bout to text you, bitch*

O

you cook pork chops same way i do, our families in another city go to the same church

O

you, rolling a blunt, holding your son, is a mecca

O

you invite me out for drag queens on the nights i think of finally [   ]

O

you pull over in Mississippi so i can walk a road my grandfather bled on

O

you gave me a stone turtle, it held your palm's scent for a week

O

i call your mama mama

O

you request like a demand, *make me some of that mango cornbread*

i cut the fruit, measure the honey

O

you & you & you & you go in on a dildo for my birthday

you name it drake, you know me

O

a year with you in that dirty house with that cracked-out cat was a good year

O

at the function, i feel myself splitting into too many rooms of static

you touch my hand & there i am

O

do you want to be best friends?

a box for yes, a box for maybe yes

O

did our grandmothers flee the fields of embers so we could find each other here?

O

friend, you are the war's gentle consequence

O

i am the prison that turns to rain in your hands

O

you, at my door the night my father leaped beyond what we know

O

the branches of silence stay heavy with your petal

O

you smell like the milk of whatever beast i am

O

your poop is news, your fart is news, your gross body my favorite bop

O

you, drunk as an uncle, making all kinds of nonsense sense

i fluent the language between your words

O

& when we fight, not a ring, but a room with no exit

we spill the blood & bandage the wound, clean cuts with tongues

O

if luck calls your name, we split the pot

& if you wither, surely i rot

O

we hate the same people, say *nigga please* with the same mouth

O

& before we were messy flesh, i'm sure we were the same dust

O

everywhere you are is a church & i am the pastor, the deacons, the mothers
fainting at the altar

O

as long as i am a fact to you, death can do with me what she wants

O

my body, water, your body, a trail of hands carrying the river to the sea

O

i ink your name into my arm to fasten what is already there

O

you made coming out coming in from the storm

O

i would love you even if you killed God

O

you are the country i bloody the hills for

O

you love me despite the history of my hands, their mangled confession

O

God bless you who screens my nudes, drafts my break-up text

O

you are the drug that knocks the birds from my heart

O

o the horrid friends who were just ships harboring me to you

O

& how many times have you loved me without my asking?

how often have i loved a thing because you loved it?

including me

O

O

with yo ugly ass

O

at the end of the world, let there be you

O

my world

more notes & more acknowledgments

"niggas!" augments a line from Ladan Osman's "How to Make a Shadow."

"how many of us have them?" borrows its title and opening from Whodini's "Friends" and includes a reference to Project Pat's "Don't Save Her."

"self-portrait as '90s R&B video" is loosely inspired by the music video for Tamia's "Stranger in My House."

The end of "my bitch!" is a gesture to the ending of Nicole Sealey's "Object Permanence."

"C.R.E.A.M." is after Wu-Tang Clan's song of the same title and Morgan Parker's poem "ALL THEY WANT IS MY MONEY, MY PUSSY, MY BLOOD."

"acknowledgments" includes segments inspired by commenters on a Facebook post where I asked people when they knew their best friend was indeed their best friend.

//

Thank you to the following publications and their editors, teams, and readers for giving early drafts of these poems their first homes and their gracious support of the work:

Adroit Journal—self-portrait as a '90s R&B video
BOAAT Journal—all the good dick lives in Brooklyn Park
The Collagist—shout out to my niggas in Mexico, saw a video of a gang of bees
    swarming a hornet who killed their bee-homie so i called to say i love you
The Fight and The Fiddle—the fat one with the switch, niggas!
Freeman's—what was said at the bus stop
Harvard Divinity Journal—old confession & new
Homology Lit—rose, gay cancer
Hyperallergic—my nig
Into—the flower who bloomed thru the fence in grandmama's yard
Los Angeles Review of Books—waiting on you to die so i can be myself
Narrative—happy hour

The New Yorker—undetectable

The Paris Review—my bitch!

Poem-A-Day—in lieu of a poem, i'd like to say, say it with your whole black
    mouth, C.R.E.A.M.

Poetry—how many of us have them?, jumped!, dogs!, sometimes i wish i felt
    the side effects, broke n rice, notes, acknowledgments

The Rumpus—for Andrew, ode to gold teeth

The Sun—trees!

Waxwing—on faggotness

Broadside Press released a broadside of "fall poem."

    //

Thank you to Jeff Shotts and Parisa Ebrahimi for your vision, your candor, your
green pen blessings, and your friendship, dear editors.

Thank you to the entire team at Graywolf Press and Chatto & Windus, mighty
offices filled with amazing women, a few great dudes, and wonderful people all
around. It is an honor to be on your teams.

Thank you to every friend, old and new, whose names and memories populate this
book. I love you all, all y'all asses. You are what keeps me here. My life will be to
repay you.

Thank you to the National Endowment for the Arts and the Montalvo Arts Center
for their generous support, which helped make space to create this work.

Thank you to my family: Mom & Fred, B & LeBron & Natalie, Grandma, Bril,
Dad (the original Smith poet), Aisha & Malik & Keisha, every cousin & uncle &
especially the aunties. To be a Smith on both sides is a mighty blessing. All my love.

To the readers: you are why we do this. Thank each of you for considering the
work, for sharing books with your friends, for continuing to make books better
than gold. As always, this book is yours now.

Thank you, God.

DANEZ SMITH is the author of *Don't Call Us Dead*, winner of the Forward Prize for Best Collection and a finalist for the National Book Award, and *[insert] boy*, winner of the Kate Tufts Discovery Award. They live in Minneapolis.

The text of *My Nig* is set in Ten Oldstyle. Book design and composition by Bookmobile Design & Digital Publisher Services, Minneapolis, Minnesota. Manufactured by Sheridan on acid-free, 30 percent postconsumer wastepaper.